The Giant's Causeway
A Remnant of Chaos

Philip S Watson

D1342417

Sponsored jointly by Environment Service and the National Trust

BELFAST : HMSO

© *Crown copyright 1992*
Applications for reproduction should be made to HMSO
First published 1992

ISBN 0 337 08300 2

The National Trust
Rowallane House
Saintfield
Ballynahinch
Co. Down BT24 7LH

Telephone: (0238) 510721

ENVIRONMENT SERVICE
Department of the Environment
   for Northern Ireland

Calvert House, 23 Castle Place
Belfast BT1 1FY

Telephone: (0232) 230560

Contents

Preface

'When the world was moulded and fashioned out of formless chaos, this must have been the bit over – a remnant of chaos!'

The title for this book is taken from this comment by William Makepeace Thackeray, following his traumatic boat trip to view the Giant's Causeway on a stormy day in October 1842.

One hundred and fifty years since Thackeray's experience, and three hundred since the Bishop of Derry and a Cambridge scholar stumbled upon the Causeway – this intrepid pair being credited with the discovery of the site – it is appropriate to publish a brief natural and cultural history of this world famous landscape. Equally appropriate is the fact that the National Trust, owner and manager of the Giant's Causeway, has nominated 1992 as Landscape Year.

Thackeray remarked of the whiskey seller at the Wishing Well by the Causeway: 'She has no change for a shilling: she never has; but her whiskey is good.' It could be said he had sampled the spirit of the place!

This book attempts to capture that other, more elusive, spirit of the Giant's Causeway. However, the full story would fill a much larger volume. This slim one is written to complement existing booklets, and should interest those who wish to delve a little deeper into the considerable range of topics to be explored at this National Nature Reserve and World Heritage Site.

The Giant's Causeway (Irish Grid reference C 946447) is situated on the north coast of County Antrim 3 km north of the town of Bushmills.

Access is off the B 146 road; O.S. N.I. map sheet 5 of the 1:50 000 series is useful. The Causeway itself is always open to pedestrians – the Visitor Centre and other visitor facilities are open at popular times.

Philip S. Watson
May 1992

Acknowledgements

My main debt of gratitude is to the National Trust, for enabling me to work at such a wonderful place, for providing support for this book and for the use of papers.

The Department of the Environment for Northern Ireland (Environment Service), also provided financial support towards publication for which I am grateful, and I wish to thank two members of staff, Dr Andrew Stott and Mike Hartwell, for assistance with the text revision and advice on illustrations.

Certain individuals – colleagues within the National Trust and others – kindly read the manuscript and made helpful comments: Ian McQuiston, Jo Whatmough, Professor Ronnie Buchanan and John Stewart Watson.

Thanks are due to the Ulster Folk and Transport Museum for access to John MacLaughlin's Causeway logbook and to Dr David Erwin of the Ulster Museum who kindly allowed me to examine various marine biology reports.

Many local people in the townlands around the Giant's Causeway gave generously of their time and hospitality, and provided a wealth of information – my thanks to them all, and in particular to David and Rose Hutchinson, the late Robert Hutchinson and Samuel Gault.

In HMSO, Dan Connor, Walter Roberts, Ruth Bowden and Alison Beaumont were most supportive throughout the production of this book.

Finally, but not least, my wife Kay has tolerated this obsession with a collection of odd-shaped stones for many years, and I thank her sincerely for suffering my absences, both on the Causeway coast and in my study.

1

Giants or Geology?

VISITORS TO THE GIANT'S CAUSEWAY have faced this choice for three hundred years. These strange rock formations beg the question of their origin, and two explanations are offered: the local legend and the scientific theory.

Most of this book is based on environmental and historical studies, but it is worth beginning in the realms of mystery and romance – with the legends and folklore that surround the Causeway's popular creator, the giant Finn MacCool.

Birth of a Legend

Before there were geologists, no natural explanation was available for the existence of the Giant's Causeway. Therefore it is not surprising that local guides created and perpetuated stories accrediting this massive pavement to the works of a giant.

Other formations of columnar basalt, the material of the Causeway, occur in various parts of the world and have been named in awe of giants or more sinister forces. For examples, a Pavé des Géants in France, the Devil's Postpile in California and Pooningbah, an Australian aboriginal site in New South Wales, also known as the Giant's Causeway, but in this case associated with a legendary giant spiny anteater.

When a party including Sir Joseph Banks, explorer and naturalist, discovered and publicised a similar phenomenon on the island of Staffa off south-west Scotland in 1772, this was interpreted by the Irish storytellers as further confirmation of Finn MacCool's activities; the columns of rock emerging from the sea at Fingal's Cave on Staffa must be the other end of the Giant's Causeway, which they believed once joined Ireland and Scotland.

The tales of giants offered to the public by the imaginative Causeway guides were met with either amused tolerance or curt dismissal. The Rev Dr William Hamilton, an eighteenth-century naturalist and author of one of the first accurate geological accounts of the Causeway area, was tolerant. In 1786 he wrote:

> The native inhabitants of this coast, as they were the earliest observers of this wonder, so they were the first to account for its production; and however rude and simple their theory may be, yet a little consideration will satisfy us, that it does not deserve the ignominious appellation of being grossly barbarous and absurd.

Another writer, a Mr Morrison who signed himself as an architect of Clonmell, in Tipperary, dismissed local opinion in 1793:

A Tale of Two Giants

Long ago an Irish giant named Finn MacCool roamed the north coast where he could look across the narrow sea of Moyle to Scotland, home of his great rival Benandonner, who challenged his strength and reputation. As the two giants had never met, Finn decided to invite Benandonner to Ireland, to engage in a decisive battle.

Being an hospitable and clever giant, Finn built a causeway of huge stones across the water so that the Scottish giant could travel on dry land, and thus find no excuse to avoid the confrontation.

However, as Benandonner approached, Finn realised to his horror that his opponent was a larger and more fiercesome rival than he had anticipated. He fled to his house in the nearby hills, and confided his fears to Oonagh, his wife. Oonagh, a practical woman, disguised Finn as a baby, complete with large nightgown and bonnet. She placed him in a huge hastily constructed cradle, and advised him to remain silent and feign sleep as Benadonner's great shadow fell across the door.

Oonagh brought the Scottish giant in for tea, pleading with him to keep quiet or he would disturb Finn's child. Looking at the massive 'baby' lying in the cradle, Benandonner took fright and, exclaiming that if this was the child, then he had no wish to meet the father, fled back to Scotland, ripping up the causeway in fear of the awful Finn pursuing him home.

The usual attempts to explain the origin of the phenomenon appear to me to be very absurd; it has its name from the ignorant credulity of the unlettered and superstitious.

Love them or hate them, the stories of the giant have survived.

The measure of a mythical giant - the Giant's Boot.

These are the reasons, claim the legend, that it is known as the Giant's Causeway, and those who remain sceptical are shown the open water with Scotland on the horizon, and a pile of broken columns which mark the destructive haste of the fleeting giant.

Finn MacCool: History or Fable?

Finn's name is immortalised in placenames throughout the Celtic fringe of the British Isles, but the embroidering of folk tales has distorted his exploits. The myths of pre-Christian Ireland survived in oral tradition and were written down in the post-Christian period. Much has been published to argue the case for accepting Finn as a possible figure of ancient history, or dismissing him as a myth.

History or fable, the Finnian tales are part of the Ossian cycle of Irish storytelling, describing the adventures of Finn and his Fianna, a band of warriors he reputedly led in the service of King Cormac mac Airt in third-century Ireland. Finn loved to hunt in the forests and hills with his faithful hounds, and his exploits remain popular today as both childrens' stories and material for scholarly Celtic studies.

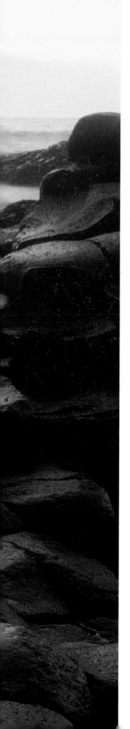

2

A Remnant of Chaos

LEAVING ASIDE FOLKLORE AND BELIEFS, the alternative explanation of the Giant's Causeway is an elemental story of earth, fire, water and wind moulding a landscape, the origins of which have been debated by scientists in confrontations equal to those of giants.

A Brief History of the Earth

By the mid-nineteenth century, the volcanic origin of the Causeway was widely accepted. One visitor made his views quite clear:

> The guide performed his office satisfactorily and most obligingly but it would be an improvement if guides could be brought to describe natural appearances correctly and omit the senseless jargon about Giants.

This dry comment was entered in the logbook of Causeway guide John MacLaughlin by the President of the Geological Society of Glasgow during his visit on 7 April 1876.

However, to describe the natural appearances of the basalts of these cliffs, bays and headlands requires an appreciation of the physical forces operating over a period of 60 million years. In geological terms, this is relatively recent, bearing in mind the accepted age of the Earth is about 4.5 billion years.

To cope with these unimaginable timescales, and to understand why the word 'recent' is appropriate, it is helpful to adapt the popular analogy used to depict the history of the Earth since its formation as represented by a single calendar year. Thus with our planet condensing from gases and dust in the first minutes of New Year's Day, one day becomes 12.6 million years. On this scale, life began in the first week of May, 3,000 million years ago. The oldest rocks bounding the Causeway coast to west and east, the schists of north Donegal and north-east Antrim (600 million years old) appeared in mid-November. Dinosaurs were roaming the area in the week before Christmas (about 150 million years ago) and the vivid white chalk (over 100 million years old) neighbouring the Causeway cliffs emerged from the sea on Christmas Eve. The Causeway lavas (55 million years old) were cooling on 27 December, and Man arrived about ten minutes before midnight on New Year's Eve.

The latter is an intimidating thought, standing on the Giant's Causeway on a clear day when, from the Inishowen peninsula of Donegal in the west to the columns below one's feet, a single glance can take in a rocky landscape spanning 600 million years of Earth history.

Creation of the Causeway Landscape

The Causeway's story began when the age of the dinosaurs was over, and a gently undulating landscape of forests growing on the Cretaceous chalk began to tremble under the force of earthquakes. This was part of great movements of the Earth's crust, as the Atlantic Ocean was forming and the land masses of Europe and the Americas were becoming further separated. A period of intense volcanic activity began in the north Atlantic, creating large areas of basalt as the outpourings of lavas cooled to solid rock.

In what is now north-east Antrim and south-west Scotland, explosive volcanic activity was an indication of the chaos to follow. Fissures in the Earth's crust appeared and lava was extruded, pouring over the land. Periods of relative quiet occurred between the many eruptions

The result was a layering of basalts, marked by bands of red laterite (from the Latin *later*, a brick) which are evidence of the breaks in volcanic activity. During these quiescent periods, the upper parts of the solidified lava flows weathered under the influence of tropical wet and dry seasons, forming the red, brown, purple and greyish bands which make up the interbasaltic beds. Apart from the metal ores contained in these (mainly iron and bauxite), occasional strips of lignite – decayed plant material also known as 'brown coal' – can still be seen.

Reddish laterite near the Giant's Harp.

This 'sandwich cake' layering was recognised by the Causeway guides, who eventually began to acquire some geological knowledge, for they often referred to 'trap' rock. The word 'trap' in this context is based on a Swedish word meaning 'stair' – an apt description of the stepped Causeway coast landscape.

A prominent dyke near Port na Spaniagh.

Further lavas were forced through existing basalts, and many of these intrusions survive as wall-like dykes or hard ridges which extend into the sea in the Causeway bays, and in some cases are evident as vertical wedges of very dark rock in the cliffs. The same process disrupted existing rocks of various types elsewhere on this coast, and created horizontal sharp-featured sills, examples being Ramore Head at Portrush, the Skerries islands offshore, Sheep Island off Ballintoy and the massive profile of Fair Head, the north-east corner of Ireland. These intruded rocks are of a different chemical composition to the extruded layers, and are thus different in colour and durability.

Over a period of several million years, this volcanic chaos produced the bones of today's Causeway landscape. Then the fiery spells ended, although faulting and other earth movements displaced some rock layers, a process which helped provide the varied structure and scenery visitors now enjoy along this coast.

Three major series of basalts exist in this area. The oldest are the Lower Basalts, visible as dark horizontal bands from sea level to the first extensive red bed of laterite. These coarser grained rocks did not form precise columns. The next extrusion of lavas poured over the weathered top of the Lower Basalts, filling hollows and cascading in fiery torrents over ledges, engulfing the forests that had become established on the red soils.

From Chaos to Order

Cracks and columns are obvious features at the Giants's Causeway, but how did this phenomenon actually form?

The runny lavas which became part of the Middle Basalt series poured into a hollow, filling what is thought to have been an earlier river valley. As cooling progressed through this volcanic pond, shrinking in the very fine grained material formed columns, irregular near the top of the flow and much more precise in the lower region. Under perfect cooling conditions, at a very even rate, this process tends to produce hexagonal structures — an efficient way to fill a space.

As the cooling rate varied, this created four-five-seven-eight and even a few nine-sided exceptions to the hexagonal rule. Tensions caused by differential cooling and shrinking within the columns split these into regular tablets of stone, the curved joints fitting together in a ball-and-socket arrangement. This is a major feature of the surface of the Causeway, noticeable as domes and hollows.

From any viewpoint on the raised castellation of the Middle Causeway, known as the Honeycomb, evidence of the former ponding of lava is noticeable as tilted columns around the rim. There are almost horizontal columns in the grassy hillside, and the Grand Causeway is clearly tilted towards the observer, while to the west, the Little Causeway shows a distinct lean to the east.

Elsewhere, irregular features are evident in the lava flows forming he Middle Basalt series, but there are many fine examples of columnar basalt in the various flows east to Benbane Head.

A final series of extruded lavas created the Upper Basalts over another thick inter-basaltic bed. These have been eroded at the Causeway area but can be seen outcropping inland, and at the coast west of Portrush.

Many visitors are tempted to conclude that the Causeway lava streams cooled in the sea, perhaps splitting the rocks into columns. Lava cooling in the sea can produce formations known as 'pillow lavas', but not columns. Pillow lavas are not found here, because at the time of these volcanic activities sea level was much lower, and the Causeway was not yet part of a coastline.

Although such extensive cross-sections are rare global features, there are numerous other, largely vertical, examples of columnar basalts in many countries. The Giant's Causeway is not unique, but the precise nature of the exposed columns, and the other readily accessible geological features, together with its well documented history of study and debate, make it worthy indeed of the wide recognition it has received.

Scientific Debates

Disagreements concerning the origins of basalts and igneous rocks in general raged across Europe in the late-eighteenth century. Three schools of thought developed: those who believed oceanic sediments formed the basis of such rocks became labelled as Neptunists. Opposed to these ideas were the Vulcanists, supporting fiery origins. Developers of this igneous theme, relying on theories of subterranean heat, fell into the camp of the Plutonists.

Geological controversies were not unusual in the seventeenth and eighteenth centuries as scientists, philosophers and naturalists developed theories on the origin of the Earth's rocks. By the mid–1820s, the views of the Vulcanists were finally accepted, and the Causeway became firmly established as a remnant of a chaotic period in the Earth's history.

"Sandwich Cake" - layers of basalts divided by a red inter-basaltic bed, at Pleaskin Head.

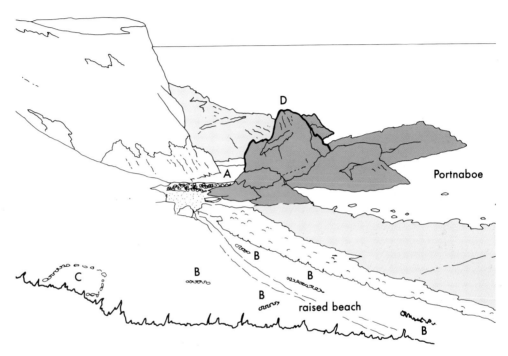

Physical features in Portnaboe: A, Brenther Port. B, Kelp walls (disused). C, Sheep fold (disused). D, the Camel dyke.

3
Time and Tide

MANY VISITORS, IN A HURRY TO SEE the Causeway, miss a surrounding landscape of extraordinary beauty and great interest. The network of paths takes the walker along routes where, with a little help, it is possible to read the landscape and understand something of the changes wrought by erosive forces.

Nature's Architects

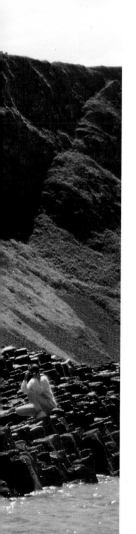

Ice and the sea were major architects in the creation of this coastline. The Atlantic Ocean continues to nibble at the shoreline and cliffs, while severe storms and huge seas from time to time take large bites from the land.

> While the Causeway itself is spectacular, so too is its setting, in the amphitheatre of the glacial and marine hewn cliffs.

Thus Professor Bill Carter, in his contribution to *The Book of the Irish Countryside (1987)*, refers to the end of the previous glacial period 15,000 years ago as the time when the Causeway coast began to develop its present shape. Further changes took place, particularly in the past 6,000 years following a peak in sea level, including the formation of coastal dunes.

These glacial periods, known as Ice Ages, locked up vast amounts of water as ice, and sea level dropped worldwide. The ice was of considerable thickness over this area, and its weight caused the land to sink. When the ice eventually melted, the land rose but so did sea level, as the water that was once ice was released.

Reading the Causeway Landscape

Complex falling and rising of sea and land over several million years left recognisable features in the bays and around the headlands of the Causeway area, although some are now hidden by scree slopes or covered with vegetation.

It would be wrong to assume that this is a static coastline; changes take place all the time, some almost imperceptible such as a trickle of small stones from cliff faces, and minor soil slippages. Other natural events are more spectacular, for example the rock fall of January 1987, when many hundreds of tonnes of columns dropped from the cliffs of the amphitheatre above Port Reostan, and shattered across the path and in the bay below. This occurred during a period of unusually severe frost, followed by a quick thaw. The columns may have split from the cliff as seeping water froze and expanded behind them. The gap remains visible as a break in an almost symmetrical row of columns near the cliff top, like missing teeth in an otherwise perfect smile.

Platforms of basalt, many with isolated rock stacks of a more resistant nature, exist where previously higher sea levels enabled the waves to cut into weaker areas of the Lower Basalts, and the higher cliff line has crumbled due to weathering processes. Raised beaches of cobbles and boulders, many covered with vegetation, and steep scree slopes are further clues for landscape detectives to spot along this dynamic coast.

Here and there rock stacks and platforms have become separated from the mainland to form small islands, while others were once joined to peninsulas, forming arches where the sea cut through the base. A good example is the promontory known as the 'King and his Nobles' near Pleaskin Head, where the outermost pillar, the 'King', was one side of a perfect arch joining the 'Nobles', until this collapsed in 1949.

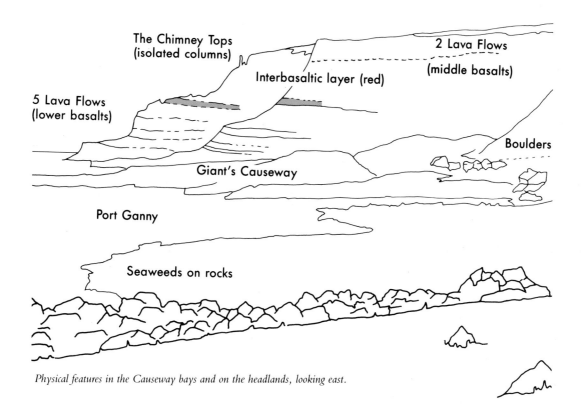

Physical features in the Causeway bays and on the headlands, looking east.

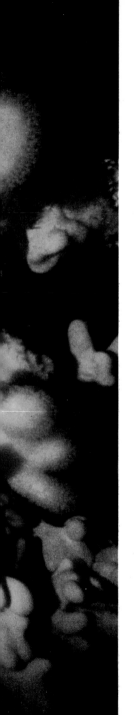

4

Living on the Coast:Wildlife

WHEN THE ICE AGE GLACIERS RETREATED, the Causeway coast, with bare rock scraped and scarred by ice, and other areas filled with deposits of glacial gravel, clay and sand, was all new territory for plants and animals to colonise.

This chapter is mostly about the flora and fauna of the land, but it begins with an account of the rich marine life in the coastal waters.

Marine Life

To present-day visitors and residents, life in the sea is not immediately obvious, except to the subaqua diver or the fishermen who make a living from marine resources. But there is much to interest the patient observer, and the dark head of a seal or the clamour of seabirds may catch the attention of the casual visitor.

The prevailing westerly winds blow across great distances in the north Atlantic Ocean, and waves driven by the Atlantic swell sweep up sandy beaches and crash on to the nearby rocky shores. Offshore, strong tides races produce short, choppy waves, and further west, an ocean front – a meeting of waters of different temperature and salinity – develops in summer between north Donegal and the Scottish island of Islay. The sea is not a uniform habitat, and these variations provide zones rich in marine plant and animal life.

Marine mammals occur in these coastal waters at most times of the year, but are more likely to be seen in summer, when the surface water is warmer and there is an abundance of food. The large Atlantic grey seal is the most frequently observed mammal, usually seen singly or in very small groups. This species is widely distributed, and the seals wander into the bays around the Causeway area to hunt for fish. The smooth dog-like head rising out of the water, or sometimes just a whiskered snout, is often all that is visible. Grey seals sometimes haul out on rocky platforms or islands, such as the bouldery base of Sheep Island facing Ballintoy.

Despite its name, the common seal is scarce along this north coast, and it is therefore the grey which can be a nuisance to salmon fishermen when it is tempted to raid the fixed nets inshore, and take advantage of the trapped fish for a few bites, or a complete meal. Other marine mammals, usually occurring further offshore, include the common porpoise, various species of dolphin and some of the smaller whales. The staff of the Environment Service's Countryside Centre at Portrush would appreciate any sightings of whales or dolphins, whether at sea or washed ashore dead, being reported to them to help in their scientific work.

Very occasionally in summer, the huge, slow-moving form of the basking shark may be seen. This should not be confused with marine mammals, for it is a fish, and a harmless feeder on tiny marine plankton.

Shoals of fish and concentrations of other marine organisms, occurring inshore in summer, attract feeding flocks of seabirds. Many of these birds come from island breeding sites at the Skerries, Sheep Island, Carrick-a-Rede, Rathlin and Ailsa Craig. Species to look out for include gannet, Manx shearwater, fulmar, kittiwake and various other gulls, razorbill, guillemot and sometimes smaller numbers of puffin, terns and skuas.

There are rich communities of plants and animals underwater, associated with the variety of submarine habitats such as cliff faces, isolated rock pinnacles, boulder beds and the dappled light and shade of the waving forests of kelp and other large seaweeds.

Sponges, hydroids, anemones, crustaceans and fish are only part of this world hidden from most visitors, but they are as equally worthy of conservation as the land based flora and fauna.

The area between the tides is a difficult zone for living organisms, for these have to cope with inundation by sea water followed by exposure to the air as tides rise and fall, as well as the pounding of the waves and the attentions of both marine and terrestrial predators.

Causeway stones - hexagons and pentagons predominate.

Plants and Animals on the Seashore

At low tide, the glistening stems and fronds of the large brown seaweeds generally known as kelp are visible where the sea meets the land. A progression of other marine algae up the shore includes serrated, bladder, spiral and channelled wracks in that order. Where fresh water reaches the upper shore from springs and streams, vivid green patches of Enteromorpha form slippery mats over the rocks.

Limpet, common mussel and species of barnacles cling to the rocks, and various periwinkles and the colourful top shell are found on the middle and upper shore.

At the splash zone – frequently dashed with salt spray – a black coating of tar lichen resembles oil pollution, but is in fact a natural growth over the rocks. Areas of vivid orange, yellow and grey lichens coat the rocks as the inter-tidal zone ends and the terrestrial area begins.

Wildlife of the Nature Reserve

In 1987 an area of 71 hectares and about 5 km in length, including the Giant's Causeway, was designated a National Nature Reserve. Although the geological features are of prime importance, the variety of plants and animals adds to the interest.

To most visitors, birds and wild flowers are the most obvious features of the natural history of the Causeway, especially in spring and summer. Although much remains to be learned about the flora and fauna of the area, surveys and casual observations have shown that this north facing coastal strip has a surprising richness of wildlife.

The seabirds feeding offshore have already been highlighted. Several of the species mentioned nest on the Causeway cliffs, but not in as large and busy colonies as found on the various islands off this coast.

The vegetation in the bays shelters a range of small birds. The most noticeable is the stonechat, and wrens are numerous, their loud song echoing around the amphitheatres of cliffs. Meadow and rock pipits are small brown birds, difficult to identify, and the song of the skylark can be heard from February to July above the cliff-top grasslands. In spring and summer, small warblers visit the low scrub, mainly the whitethroat.

On the shore, the piping of the black and white oystercatcher and the call of the curlew reveal the presence of these waders, and in the spring and autumn migration periods, as well as through the winter, they are joined by turnstone, redshank and the occasional purple sandpiper.

Stonechat on whin.

Male eider on the sea.

In the bays, look out for the large eider, a sea duck. The male is black and white for most of the year, and the female brown. In June and July, females lead flotillas of tiny ducklings which bob fearlessly in the surf.

The land mammals are less easily seen, but it is worth being alert for the presence of the large russet Irish hare on the grasslands and rougher grazings inland. The stoat (the weasel does not occur in Ireland) may be seen occasionally, hunting prey amongst the stones of the scree slopes. Both fox and badger occur, the former quite frequently but the latter is more often found a little way inland, where

Birds on the Causeway Cliffs

The many ledges and tops of columns along the cliffs are taken over by the noisy fulmar from December to August. These large gull-like birds are members of the petrels, an oceanic group. The adults dispute their cliff sites with neighbours through the winter, coming and going until the female lays her single egg in May. The young bird leaves in late August, and the cliffs are silent until the fulmars return after a period of feeding in the Atlantic, which takes them as far away as the Newfoundland Banks.

Other coastal nesting birds making use of cliffs and caves are the shag, a slimmer version of the cormorant, which itself nests further east in a large colony on Sheep Island, and the little black guillemot. The latter has its stronghold around the Runkerry cliffs west of the Causeway Centre, and in summer plumage is unmistakable with its black body, white wing patches and vermilion legs and feet. The herring gull breeds in medium-sized colonies on the rock platforms and small islands and, in the caves, sharing the dark recesses with the occasional shag, is the rock dove, looking not unlike a street pigeon.

The cliffs are also home to raven, jackdaw, starling, kestrel and peregrine falcon, and the fortunate observer may catch a glimpse of that red-billed, red-legged crow, the chough, now very rare in Northern Ireland.

it makes setts in old field banks and ditches. Sometimes its habits of prowling at night and following regular pathways often lead it into danger on the roads. The tiniest mammal in this island is the pygmy shrew and, although rarely seen, its high pitched squeaks can be heard in summer in the tall grasses.

Natural Rockeries

The vigour and colour of the flowers and shrubs bring the dark cliffs and grassy slopes to life with a flourish in spring and summer. Almost 200 species have been recorded in the nature reserve, and the months of May and June are best for the flowering of the wind- and salt-tolerant plants which hug the shores, slopes and cliffs, turning the coastline into a continuous rock garden.

Cushions of sea pink or thrift mingle with the pure white sea campion, and a variety of shades characterise the latter's relative, the red campion – from deep red through pink to almost white – and the yellow of bird's-foot trefoil blends with the lemon shade of kidney vetch.

Throughout the year there is usually some colour, for most species have distinctive flowering periods, and deep in the sheltered bays primrose and sea campion may be found in bloom even in midwinter, defying the seasonal rule.

Other Wildlife

Few trees are found on this exposed Causeway area, except where groups of Sycamore or other wind-tolerant species have been planted to give shelter around farmsteads. Salty winds and nibbling sheep make life difficult for seedlings trying to establish themselves on the coastal strip.

Plants provide food and shelter for many insects. Butterflies are obvious on warm days in spring and summer, with the tiny common blue, usually found on its food plant, bird's-foot trefoil. Bare ground will attract grayling on sunny days, and the occasional red admiral and peacock pass through in summer and early autumn.

Rotting seaweed on the shore is home and larder in the life cycle of kelp flies. These are harmless insects, but large hatches can result in irritating numbers clustering around picnickers and at car windows. However, insect hatches provide abundant food for some birds, and also for predatory insects such as the orange soldier beetle, usually to be seen on the umbrella-shaped creamy flower heads of hogweed.

Habitats and Communities

A number of plant names have been given already, but the individual plants live in habitats and as communities that the botanist and ecologist will recognise as adaptions to the varying conditions imposed by the maritime location, and other factors. Tolerance of the drying effect of salty winds is vital, and the shade under the towering cliffs encourages a number of species more commonly found in woodland, such as wood anemone, violets and ferns.

Fresh water seeps between layers of basalt and there are numerous springs and rivulets, resulting in marshy patches on the raised beaches and other flat areas near the shore, where orchids and the tall yellow flag iris can be found.

Fragments of salt marsh exist near high water mark, and patches of bramble and blackthorn scrub add to the habitats below the cliffs. The narrow cliff-top strip contains clumps of low wind-pruned whin, including western gorse, heaths and heathers, with early purple, spotted and fragrant orchids. Maritime grassland is a scarce and important habitat existing here, with communities typified by spring squill and catspaw – the latter providing a delightful carpet of white and pink flowers in early summer.

These habitats and their plant communities are extremely valuable in terms of nature conservation, a point emphasised by the proximity of the intensively managed farm-land, which has replaced most of the heaths and wilder grasslands which once covered these cliff headlands.

5

Living on the Coast: People

MANY OF THE NATURAL RESOURCES of this coast were useful to the first settlers who arrived around 9,000 years ago. They fashioned tools and weapons from the flint of the chalky shores and had a keen eye for outcrops of hard rocks to make stone axes. The abundance of wildlife provided food and skins and gradually woodlands were cleared to provide firewood, shelter and, eventually, areas to farm.

Today, fishing, farming and the tourist business are the main occupations of coastal people who depend to some extent on natural resources, but many traditional occupations and activities have ceased.

Forgotton Places

Although there is little surviving evidence, the earliest settlers in Ireland, the Mesolithic and Neolithic people of the Stone Age cultures between approximately 9,000 and 4,000 years ago, probably made use of these rocky shores and cliff-bound bays for fishing and collecting seabirds' eggs. Along the coast, a little way inland, the Neolithic people buried their dead in the family tombs known as megaliths. Their settlements have been found at nearby Mount Sandel on the river Bann upstream from Coleraine, and in the dunes of Portstewart and at Whitepark Bay.

Scattered about the countryside near the Causeway are the raths (farmsteads with enclosing earth banks) and souterrains (underground storage and hiding places) of the late Iron Age and Early Christian periods. Early indications of human presence at the Causeway shores are found in placenames and oral traditions.

Placenames

The little cove known as the Brenther, within Portnaboe (immediately below the Giant's Causeway Centre) takes its name from the Norse, meaning 'Steep Harbour'. A tradition survives here that the Vikings camped under their upturned longboat, raised on stones to provide a makeshift shelter.

Further east is the jagged rock stack of Benadanir, the 'Peak of the Danes'. These connection with Norsemen, Danes or Viking are tenuous, for there is little direct evidence of Viking presence on this section of coast, despite the evocative placenames. Vikings stormed Dunseverick Castle in 870 AD and archaeological finds associated with them have been recorded on other parts of the coast and at Rathlin Island.

The Story of Kelp

Although a useful fertiliser, especially for potato crops, the main use for the brown seaweeds was for kelp production. Kelp is the general name for the large brown algae of the lower shore and subtidal zone, but it was also the term applied to the burned product of these seaweeds, once they had been collected and dried.

The thick-stemmed oarweeds and other brown algae that form underwater 'forests' in these relatively clear Atlantic waters grow most vigorously in spring and summer. In winter, the weakened and dead stems and fronds are washed ashore in large quantities during gales and in periods of large swells. In May, the 'Cuckoo storms' throw up further piles which are known locally as the 'May fleece'. These banks of seaweed lie rotting today, providing nutrients for seashore plants, but from the eighteenth century to the 1930s, this inshore bounty was collected by Causeway coast fishermen and farmers and their families during winter and spring, and stacked to dry over small stone walls constructed for this purpose near the tideline. In some areas the algae were cut fresh from their holdfasts in shallow water, but around the Causeway, the seaweed was collected along the shore.

The kelp walls survive in Portnaboe, and in several bays to the east. When the seaweed had been dried, it was laid on iron bars over stone-lined pits or kelp kilns, and burned. The molten residue eventually cooled and hardened to a bluish rock-like substance called kelp. The kelp was sold through agents, and most of the Causeway coast production was shipped from Ballycastle to Scotland, where it was marketed with the kelp from the Scottish coast and western isles.

Kelp money was an important part of the annual income of Causeway coast people. Salts of sodium and potassium from kelp were useful in bleaching processes and in making soap and glass. The later discovery that iodine was present in kelp proved useful in medicine and photography, two applications which prolonged the industry through the late-nineteenth century.

By the 1930s, modern methods of recovering large amounts of these chemicals from other resources destroyed the demand for kelp, and even the more recent exploitation of seaweeds for the alginate industry has not revived interest in the Causeway coast's seaweed resources.

The whitish smoke of kelp fires is no longer seen, but once it was a regular feature in summer on these northern shores. While it was probably an irritant to the kelp burners, the pungent smoke was believed by some to have decongestant qualities, and local lore records that sufferers were prepared to take a lungful or two to alleviate bronchial troubles.

Magheraboy passage grave on the Causeway coast.

The bays and headlands have names derived from the Irish language, which are descriptive or linked with legends or past activities and events: Portnaboe, the port or inlet of the cow; Port Ganny, the sandy port; Port Noffer, the Giant's port; Port na Callian, the girls' port; Lacada Point, the long flagstone; Port na Spaniagh and many more.

The prefix 'Dun' in the names of stone castles or their remains, such as Dunluce and Dunseverick, refers in general to defended or perhaps fortified sites, suggesting that strategic coastal promontories may have been occupied long before the Normans and Ulster clans took over these spectacular headlands to build their castles and mansions.

Raiding Vikings, invading Normans, warring clans – all seem to have passed the Causeway by, and perhaps in those times it was not an important place, being left to the shepherds, fishermen and seaweed gatherers to lead their lives unmolested.

Making a Living

There is a continuity of activities at the Causeway traceable from the seventeenth century, for the published accounts of travellers and naturalists refer frequently to the occupations of local people.

The right to take seaweed from the tideline still exists, but it is now rarely exercised, except for the occasional load to dress the land, or the harvesting of edible species such as dulse, a red algae which, when dried, is a traditional if somewhat salty snack.

Fisheries

Catching fish and shellfish along parts of this north coast has provided food and a way of life since Mesolithic times. Near the Causeway, small ports and harbours have supported inshore fisheries for at least 300 years, and salmon continue to be fished at sites listed in the 1640s.

A particular double-ended fishing vessel, much used in the nineteenth century, was a descendant of the Norway yawl, known locally as a 'drontheim'. These were propelled by oar and sail but only modified versions survive today, most having been replaced by larger, motorised boats. The latter cannot operate as close inshore or from tiny coves and slips as successfully as did the old drontheims.

In 1926, the small harbours nearest to the Causeway, Dunseverick and Portballintrae, contained twenty working boats supporting fifty-four fishermen, including those who worked part-time.

Apart from fixed salmon nets at various shore stations, fishing was mainly for lobster, edible crab and fish living on or near the sea bed, such as cod, skate and plaice. Long lines with hundreds of baited hooks were set, or small trawls towed to catch a greater variety of species. In spring and summer, drift nets were employed further offshore to catch salmon and occasionally herring.

At the start of the nineteenth century, up to fourteen drontheims operated from Portnaboe, alternately fishing and carrying tourists to see the Causeway.

Now there are no full-time fishermen at these ports, largely due to declining fish stocks, increased freight charges and alternative employment ashore, but traditional salmon netting continues. From May to September, fixed bag nets for salmon can be seen at Portmoon and Carrick-a-Rede. The latter site, 13 km east of the Causeway, is famous for the rope bridge that the fishermen sling for access between the mainland and the island-based fishery. The name means 'Rock in the Road'; the 'road' is the swimming route of the Atlantic salmon, as the fish migrate from east to west along the coast, seeking their home rivers and spawning beds.

Drontheims hauled up in Portnaboe about the turn of the century.

Smugglers and Scavengers

This inhospitable coast, with its jagged promontories, caves, secluded coves and rocky creeks has its fair share of smugglers' tales. There are too, other stories of shipwrecks and beachcombers and the profits which resulted.

The proximity of the Scottish mainland and western isles added to the attraction of illegal exchanges. In the port of Campbeltown, only 18 km by sea from the Antrim coast, surviving customs records for the years 1739-1816 show that not all the tales of smugglers were fiction. Variation in excise duties and other taxes led to the smuggling of horses and livestock and such goods as salt, soap, hides, wool, tea and tobacco. Irish and Scotch whiskies flowed in both directions at various times.

Beachcombing – scavenging along the tideline for useful flotsam and jetsam – is a long-established activity on the Causeway. The sea continues to provide a somewhat unpredictable reward for those opportunists prepared to exploit it, whether for profit or simply as a pastime.

It is believed the Macdonnells of Dunluce improved their castle with ordnance and other pickings from the wreck of the Spanish Armada vessel, *Girona*, near the Causeway in 1588. In more recent times, two World Wars provided a range of the useful and sometimes tragic reminders of losses at sea. Ropes, timbers, apples, butter, tobacco, whiskey and the personal effects of sailors – the bounty from shipwrecks varied, and the popular but sometimes dangerous activity of wreck diving continues to add to this list today.

Mining and Quarrying

Not all commercial activities were sea and shore based. The more extensive inter-basaltic or red beds between the Lower, Middle and Upper Basalts contain varying amounts of iron and aluminium ores. These metal ores were mined from the 1860s to the 1920s, the peak extractions being in the decade 1870–1880.

Coastguard near the Causeway (Portballintrae), about 1898.

Most of the adits, or horizontal tunnels, were driven into the inter-basaltic bed between the Middle and Upper Basalts, further inland. However, there were adits in the red bed between the Lower and Middle Basalts at Port Truin and Port Fad near Portmoon. Two openings are still visible, but they are now almost inaccessible, and extremely dangerous to enter or explore. The ore taken from these mines was shipped from a hazardous berth below Contham Head – and probably joined the ores from more productive mines in east Antrim which were exported to processing plants in Britain.

The dark basalts themselves were quarried for road-building and other uses – indeed there are still working quarries in County Antrim. Outcrops of columnar basalts at various sites along the Causeway coast were also quarried, for the popular symmetrical stones used in the more decorative forms of stonemasonry.

Farming

The soils derived from the chalk and basalts of north Antrim grow good grass, and beef and dairy cattle thrive on the agriculturally improved grasslands, while sheep are grazed on both improved and rough pastures. The grassy slopes of the Causeway bays were once stocked with sheep, but this activity has ceased, except further east around the Bengore Head ('Headland of the Goats') to Portmoon area.

The intensive farming – two or three cuts of grass per season for silage, plus barley and potato crops – has had an effect on soils, landscape and wildlife. The patchwork of small fields, extending in most places to the edge of the cliffs, with small farms and clachans (traditional clustered settlements of farm buildings and dwellings), trimmed hedgerows and stone walls provides a pleasant rural landscape, but it is relatively impoverished in wildlife.

Taking Time Off

Fairs and regattas were popular events on the Causeway coast over 100 years ago, but few survive today. There was a Causeway Fair, well attended in the nineteenth century, which enjoyed a brief revival in later years. It was held in fields near the present Causeway Centre. Apart from land-based activities – sports and other competitions – one of the highlights of these get-togethers was the skiff racing.

Two- and four-oared skiffs, built specifically for sea racing, battled for honours at regattas from Donegal to east Antrim. A unique vessel surviving from these racing days in the last decades of the nineteenth century is the skiff, *Arrow*, built in Donegal for the Lochaber oarsmen (the old name for the Causeway shore). The almost legendary exploits of the *Arrow* and her crew were recorded in local newspapers, and by poets. Forgotten for over eighty years, the *Arrow* was rescued from a fishing shed in 1986, where she had been abandoned. This sleek vessel has been restored, and is on display in the Causeway Centre.

6
Worth Going to See

THE GIANT'S CAUSEWAY WAS FIRST mentioned in visitors' accounts and descriptions in the last decade of the seventeenth century.

The following quoted exchange between a great man of letters and his biographer does the Causeway an injustice:

Boswell to Dr Johnson: 'Is not the Causeway worth seeing?'
Johnson's answer: 'Aye, worth seeing; but not worth going to see.'

The number and variety of visitors in the past 300 years is proof that the Causeway is worth going to see. However, Dr Johnson was not the only sceptic, for others made the journey and, although very much in the minority, not all found quite what they were expecting.

Discovery

Surveys and maps of Ireland published before the late-1600s did not include the Giant's Causeway, which is surprising, for some were the work of creditable naturalists and cartographers.

In the summer of 1692, the Bishop of Derry, accompanied by an un-named Cambridge graduate, visited the site, and the bishop's companion communicated his observations to Sir Richard Bulkeley, a Fellow of Trinity College in Dublin; he in turn wrote to Sir Martin Lister, President of the Royal Society. This letter was published in the Philosophical Transactions of that Society in 1693, becoming the first know account of the Causeway. Thus scientists, philosophers and naturalists were the first to take an interest in the phenomenon, and the published accounts of the late-seventeenth and early-eighteenth centuries attempted to describe the strange rock formations. The earliest illustrations were, however, both inaccurate and fanciful.

In 1740, an unknown Dublin artist, Miss Susanna Drury, spent some time on site to produce several paintings depicting the east and west prospects of the Giant's Causeway. These illustrations, and subsequent engravings of them by Vivarès were sufficiently accurate and striking to arouse the interest of many people, for the engravings were widely circulated in Europe in the latter part of the eighteenth century.

Visitors began to arrive in increasing numbers, and these travellers and tourists soon attracted the attention of local residents, who realised that the interest in their patch of coastline had commercial potential.

Boatmen, Guides and Entertainers

Generations of Causeway boatmen, guides, souvenir sellers, and others thrived for over 200 years. They were well described by John McConaghie, the National Trust's first warden of the Causeway, who recorded his impressions on audio tape in the early 1960s:

> I don't think now there are many boatmen, or combined boatmen-guides at the Giant's Causeway. But in the old days . . . there were dozens of them, and each man was a real character in his own right . . . These guides interested people with stones; entertained them with legends; instructed them in geology; showed the people what to look for, what to look at; amused them with their stories, and impressed them with the unique experience of seeing the Giant's Causeway for the first time.

Not everyone loved the guides. William Thackeray arrived on a stormy day in the autumn of 1842, gathering material for his Irish Sketch Book (1843). Bundled into a small boat, much against his better judgement, he was not impressed with his first view of the Causeway from his uncomfortable position:

> 'That's the Causeway before you', says the guide.
> 'Which?'
> 'That pier which you see jutting out into the bay, right a-head.'
> 'Mon Dieu! and have I travelled a hundred and fifty miles to see that?'

And his feeling for the boat ride:

'For after all, it must be remembered that it is pleasure we come for – that we are not obliged to take these boats. – Well, well! I paid ten shillings for mine, and ten minutes before would cheerfully have paid five pounds to be allowed to quit it;'

Harsh words! But Thackeray felt out of place on what he described as a wild and inhospitable shore, and later that stormy October day found more comfort in a meal and a good bottle of wine in Miss Henry's inn, established in 1836 and now the Causeway Hotel.

The guides had a basic but adequate knowledge of geological features, but it was in tales of Finn MacCool that they excelled. To reinforce the legends of the giant, they named prominent natural features such as the Giant's Boot, his Grandmother, his Pulpit, his Harp and Organ Pipes and many more.

Adventures and Tragedies

Popular guide books of the nineteenth century describe the boat services at the Causeway, there being two main alternatives: the 'short course' encompassed the caves west of Portnaboe and the Causeway, while the 'long course' also took the visitor east as far as Benbane Head and Portmoon, to view the wonders of the amphitheatre and it rows of columns, the magnificent colonades of Pleaskin Head, the Nurse-and-Child rock, the Lion's Head and Port-na-Spaniagh. In the latter bay are Spaniard's Rock, Spaniard's Cave and the Spanish Organ – all clues to the fateful visit by a ship of the Spanish Armada in 1588.

A Survivor's Tale

The account of one fortunate survivor, Capt Francisco de Cuellar, provided a vivid first-hand record of his shipwreck in county Sligo and his arduous journey on foot to the Causeway coast, where he escaped to Scotland and eventually reached sanctuary in Antwerp, and finally home to Spain. Many were less fortunate, including about 1,300 soldiers, sailors and noblemen on the *Girona*, and there are 'Spaniard's Rocks' around the Irish north and west coasts, marking the sites where many of the Armada ships and their men failed to reach home waters.

Salamander pendant recovered from the wreck site of the "Girona".

Spanish Treasure

In September and October 1588, the surviving ships of the Spanish Armada were struggling homewards by the long route around the north of Scotland and the Atlantic coast of Ireland. After their defeat in the English Channel, this was their only option, as the English fleet had blocked their retreat. In poor condition and encountering bad weather, at least twenty came to grief on the Irish coastline, from the Giant's Causeway to County Kerry.

In the bay below the prominent rock stacks known as the 'chimneys' on the Causeway's eastern skyline is the wreck site of the galleass Girona. With all the placename clues in Port-na-Spaniagh, it may seem surprising that the remains of the Girona were not discovered until 1967. However, finding the little that would be left of a wooden ship which foundered 400 years ago on this rocky, storm-lashed coast is not an easy task, and searchers may have been misled by historical records suggesting that this ship sank further west, nearer Dunluce Castle than Port-na-Spaniagh.

The Belgian diver and marine historian Robert Stenuit and his team carried out a thorough underwater excavation of the site each summer during the years 1967 to 1969. The fabulous treasure and artefacts recovered are retained in the Ulster Museum in Belfast, where many of the finds are on display. The collection includes items recovered from La Trinidad Valencera, another Armada wreck discovered nearby, in north Donegal, in 1971. The finds provided a great deal of knowledge of the Armada ships, of life on board, and of the men who sailed on these ill-fated vessels.

Travelling to the Causeway

A major development in transport, and a delight for visitors for over sixty years, was the Causeway tram.

In 1883, this hydro-electric tram began service along a picturesque coastal route from Portrush, past Dunluce Castle to Bushmills. In 1887, the line was extended to a terminus in the grounds of the Causeway Hotel, bringing visitors within easy reach of the Giant's Causeway.

The tram's designer and engineer, William Traill, took the power for his invention from the water of the river Bush, developing a turbine in an old mill building. The tram operated until 1949 when competition from motor cars and public road transport ended a unique experience for visitors. The rolling stock was auctioned, the lines removed, and only the route survives, marked by the occasional stumps of poles which supported lines.

An impression of the tram can be obtained by viewing a surviving saloon car and 'toast-rack carriage' in the Ulster Folk and Transport Museum, and a full size replica carriage is on display in the Causeway Centre. However, these are no substitute for the noisy, spectacular journey from Portrush to the Causeway on Traill's tram, an experience unfortunately now part of the Causeway's history.

Giant's Causeway tram (car no. 7) passing Dunluce Castle in the late 19th century.

Older residents of the Causeway area recall with nostalgia the rattling tram and crowds of visitors arriving, first in horse drawn jaunting cars, then by tram, and finally in motor cars, charabancs and coaches. Some claim that, in the inter-war years, the famous stones were covered with people, and that numbers exceeded the 350,000 or so that came in 1991. We will never know, for no visitor statistics exist for these earlier years.

The Causeway was not always an open and natural site where people could wander at will. In 1898, following an appeal in court to try to prevent enclosure, a private syndicate succeeded in leasing the Giant's Causeway from local owners. Unsightly railings were erected, a toll gate was installed and from this date to 1961 a charge was levied for access to the Causeway itself. In 1899, writer Steven Gwynn found this 'an innovation . . . which every good Irishman resents.'

This highly commercialised period may have been disliked by some, but the range of services provided for the tourist was considerable – two hotels, guides, boat trips, souvenir and curio sellers, photographers, tearoom, even a drop of whiskey to accompany your drink at the Wishing Well. There is also evidence that the syndicate brought the quarrying of Causeway stones under some control, and they created and extended cliff paths to provide the basis of today's routes.

The loss of the tram in 1949 was a blow to the already declining services at the Causeway in the years after the Second World War; in 1961 the National Trust acquired the Giant's Causeway and a new phase of conservation management commenced, leading to the modern visitor facilities now located at the cliff top.

A jaunting car leaving for the Causeway in the late 19th century.

7
Caring for the Causeway

BETWEEN 1961 AND 1964, under the chairmanship of the then Lord Antrim, the National Trust acquired the Giant's Causeway and many of the adjacent headlands and bays. In addition, agreements were made with neighbouring landowners for access permission, and a significant part of today's spectacular North Antrim Cliff Path was established.

The Trust appointed a warden, and gradually the remnants of commercial activity – railings, turnstile, buildings – were removed or relocated behind the cliff top. The Causeway was restored as near as possible to its natural state, although the access road and existing cliff paths were retained.

Developing New Facilities

Thirty years of conservation and care continue, and the increasing promotion of environmental matters, together with active marketing of the Giant's Causeway as a prime tourist site, has resulted in the present-day complex of facilities at the approach to the cliff top known as Causeway Head.

Planning of the complex began in 1980 when the Northern Ireland Tourist Board produced a report based on a survey of visitors to the Giant's Causeway. This recorded many comments, and one of particular note was the desire for modern tourist facilities to service this famous site. Subsequently, Moyle District Council, representing a scattered population along much of the Causeway coast, accepted the challenge of providing a major visitor centre, with a mixed package of funding from a number of sources. In May 1986, the Giant's Causeway Centre opened its doors to visitors and residents, and has proved to be popular, winning numerous awards. This site is shared between the Giant's Causeway Centre and adjacent car parks of Moyle District Council, the National Trust, local entrepreneurs running souvenir shops and an hotel, and the North-East Education and Library Board, who manage an Environmental Resource Centre for schoolchildren in the architecturally unusual old Causeway Schoolhouse.

Conservation and Access – a Management Challenge

The Giant's Causeway is one of the most visited sites in Ireland, a fact which provides the National Trust, as owner and manager, with a challenge to balance the requirements of visitors with the long-term conservation of the rock formations, the surrounding landscape and the flora and fauna.

Helping to meet this challenge are the conservation designations awarded to the area. In 1986 the Giant's Causeway was added to the UNESCO list of World Heritage Sites. The following year, 1987, the Department of the Environment for Northern Ireland designated 71 hectares of the coast and cliffs as a National Nature Reserve. In addition, the whole site is included in the Causeway Coast Area of Outstanding Natural Beauty, designated by the Department in 1989. Further details of these designations are given on page 48.

Thus the Giant's Causeway has, in common with some of its more distinguished visitors, a range of titles – enough to intimidate even a giant! But what do they mean? Are they merely accolades? All these designations recognise that skilful management will be required to conserve the natural and cultural heritage within their geographical boundaries. The designations confirm that Environment Service is committed to providing support, both advisory and through grant-aid, towards the conservation of the Causeway including the creation and improvement of safe access and the conducting of research studies and surveys. Other bodies, such as the Northern Ireland Tourist Board, provide means to develop and improve visitor facilities, from surveys of tourists to the provision of interpretative materials.

Threats: Past, Present and Future

The Giant's Causeway, in company with many other areas of the Irish coast and countryside, faces increasing visitor pressure and environmental changes, both local and of a wider nature.

One of the earliest problems subsequent to the site's discovery was quarrying. A Vivarès engraving, made between 1743 and 1744, of Susanna Drury's *East Prospect of the Giant's Causeway* shows scattered and broken columns below the Causeway's east face; an inscription on the engraving begins: 'This Extraordinary Quarry . . .'. The stones were sold as curios, garden ornaments and gate pillars, and many found their way overseas – a Causeway guide's logbook records a consignment ordered by an American visitor on 12 August 1867.

This damaging activity has ceased, and the rubble of broken columns that remains today is evidence of this former exploitation and not, as suggested by tales in the first chapter, the mark of a fleeing giant, although this makes a good story.

The columnar basalts at the Causeway have resisted the forces of ice and the ocean, the three promontories being separated by channels where the sea has gradually cut through areas of weakness. Studies of photographs over the past 100 years have shown that a number of individual columns within the existing formations have suffered damage or removal of parts. The nature and position of such damage suggest vandalism, or careless treatment by people, but regular warden patrols and educational activities are discouraging such activities.

The possibility of rising sea level poses more of a threat to access than structure, as the Causeway has been under water before. Periods of higher sea-level in the past helped to carve the escalloped coastline evident today, and further erosion could be expected if current predictions of climatic change prove correct.

The continuous natural erosion of the coast, and some activities of visitors and residents, pose threats to both access and conservation. Nearby agricultural operations influence soils, water, landscape, flora and fauna, while visitors exert a certain amount of wear and tear on the fabric of the paths and adjacent vegetation. Visitors who stray onto farm land can interfere with farming operations or livestock.

The observant walker on the narrow cliff-top path cannot fail to notice that the agriculturally improved grasslands and cultivated fields of the nearby farmland extend almost to the edge of the cliffs. This intensive production is maintained with high inputs of inorganic fertilisers, where once farmyard manure and seaweeds were used. The enriched land drains through small watercourses and seepage, and this flow of nutrients, together with fertilisers sometimes blowing on to the Causeway Nature Reserve during nearby application, can have a damaging effect on the flora in particular and the other wildlife in general.

In 1990, the Department of Agriculture, Northern Ireland, declared its commitment to minimise environmental damage associated with agriculture and to enhance and conserve the rural environment.

Rural development policies to keep people on the land are vital, and the success of schemes such as Environmentally Sensitive Areas, where farmers choosing to join this initiative are given advice, encouragement and grants to manage their land in sympathy with the landscape and its wildlife, will be largely dependent on how many support such voluntary programmes.

The soil slippages and rock falls that continue along this dynamic cliff-line make care of the coastal paths difficult for the National Trust. Maintaining a careful balance of low-key interference with geological features, restoration of path surfaces, drainage and limited fencing, the area is kept open and as safe as possible, without detracting from the wild and rugged Atlantic scenery that so many people come here to enjoy.

Caring for the Causeway in the future will require good planning and considerable commitment of staff and other resources. There is need for research in many environmental disciplines, as well as gathering more information on the numbers, origin, behaviour and expectations of the Causeway coast visitors.

Many interests are represented along this coastal strip: town and country planning, agriculture, fisheries, conservation of buildings, landscape and nature, archaeology, tourism and recreation. To balance these for sustainable management is the greatest challenge for the future, so that the Giant's Causeway can survive as a remnant of chaos within a landscape retaining its present natural beauty.

Reading List

Chapter 1:

M Potter, 'The Giant's Wife', in *Jackanory: Stories From Ireland*, BBC Publications, 1968.

R. Coghlan, *Pocket Dictionary of Irish Myth and Legend*, Appletree Press, 1985.

M Donnelly, *Finn MacCool* (leaflet), 1984.

W Hamilton, *Letters concerning the northern coast of the County of Antrim*, Dublin, 1786.

R Morrison, 'Observations on the Giant's Causeway in the County of Antrim', *Anthological Hibernica*, August 1793, pp 105-7.

T F O'Rahilly, *Early Irish History and Mythology*, The Dublin Institute for Advanced Studies, Dublin, 1946.

Chapter 2:

D Attenborough, *Life on Earth: A Natural History* Collins/BBC, 1979.

Department of the Environment, Northern Ireland, *UNESCO World Heritage List, Giant's Causeway: Natural Site Nomination,* Universities Press, 1985.

H E Wilson and P I Manning, *'Geological Survey of Northern Ireland,* 'Geology of the Causeway Coast, Volume 1', HMSO, 1978.

A Hallam, *Great Geological Controversies,* Oxford University Press, 1983.

The National Trust, *Giant's Causeway County Antrim.* Coast and Countryside (leaflet) series, 1982.

The National Trust, *The Story of the Causeway Stones* Colour Souvenir (booklet), 1987.

J Thackray, *The Age of the Earth*, Geological Museum, Institute of Geological Sciences, HMSO, 1980.

Ulster Folk and Transport Museum *Logbook of John MacLaughlin,* Causeway guide, 1867.

Chapter Three:

R W G Carter, *Shifting Sands, A Study of the Coast of Northern Ireland from Magilligan to Larne*, Department of the Environment for Northern Ireland, Countryside and Wildlife Research Series No. 2, HMSO, 1991.

F Mitchell, *Shell Guide to Reading the Irish Landscape*, Country House, 1986.

F Mitchell et. al., *The Book of the Irish Countryside*, The Blackstaff Press and Town House, 1987.

Chapter Four:

D G. Erwin, B E Picton, D W Connor, C M Howson, P Gilleece and M J Bogues, *Inshore Marine Life of Northern Ireland*, Department of the Environment for Northern Ireland/Ulster Museum, 1990.

Institute of Offshore Engineering, *Northern Ireland Littoral Survey, First Annual Report 1984–85. A Report to the Department of the Environment for Northern Ireland*, Herriott-Watt University, Edinburgh, 1985.

C. Lloyd, M L Tasker and K E Partridge, *The Status of Seabirds in Britain and Ireland*, T. and A D Poyser, 1991.

The National Trust, 'Biological Survey – North Antrim Coast', unpublished report, 1985.

Teachers' Centre, *Giant's Causeway Environmental Studies Project,* University of Ulster (Coleraine), 1975.

P S Watson, 'The Seabirds of Northern Ireland and Adjacent Waters', *Irish Birds*, 1980 1:462-486.

Chapter five:

C Dallat, *A Tour of the Causeway Coast, Historic Photographs from the W A Green Collection in the Ulster Folk and Transport Museum*, The Friar's Bush Press, Belfast, 1990.

C Dallat, *Antrim Coast and Glens: A Personal View*, Department of the Environment, Northern Ireland, HMSO, 1990.

Government of Northern Ireland, *Report of the Advisory Committee on the Development of Fishery Harbours in Northern Ireland,* HMSO, 1927.

F Hammond, *Antrim Coast and Glens: Industrial Heritage*, Department of the Environment Northern Ireland, HMSO, 1991.

D Harpur, 'Kelp Burning in the Glens', *The Glynns*, Journal of the Glens of Antrim Historical Society, 1974, 2:19–24.

S Henry (ed.), *Rowlock Rhymes and Songs of Exile, by 'North Antrim',* The Quota Press, 1933.

J. Irivin, 'The Campbeltown Customs Records', *The Glynns,* Journal of the Glens of Antrim Historical Society, 1976, 4:36-48.

M McCaughan, 'Double-ended and Clinker-built: the Irish Dimension of a European Boatbuilding Tradition', in *The Use of Tradition,* Ulster Folk and Transport Museum, HMSO, 1988, pp 33-48.

J P Mallory and T E McNeill, *The Archaeology of Ulster from Colonization to Plantation,* Institute of Irish Studies, Queen's University of Belfast, 1991.

J D C Marshall, *Forgotton Places of the North Coast,* Clegnagh Publishing, 1991.

J E Mullin, *The Causeway Coast,* The Universities Press (Belfast) Ltd., 1982.

P C Woodman, *Excavations at Mount Sandel, 1973–77,* Northern Ireland Archaeological Monographs: No. 2, Department of the Environment, Northern Ireland, HMSO, 1985.

Chapter Six:

H Allingham, *Captain Cuellar's Adventures in Connaght and Ulster AD 1588,* Elliot Stock, London, 1897.

Anon, *Brief on Hearing of Appeal (Giant's Causeway Dispute),* Her Majesty's Court of Appeal in Ireland. Printed by John Ferguson, Ballymoney, 2 November 1897.

M Anglesea and J Preston, 'A Philosophical Landscape: Susanna Drury and the Giant's Causeway', *Art History,* 3: 252-73, 1980.

M J Baddeley, *Thorough Guide Series, Ireland (Part One) Northern Counties,* Dulau and Co., London, 1887.

E Hardy, *Survivors of the Armada,* Constable, London, 1966.

L Flanagan. *Ireland's Armada Legacy,* Gill and MacMillan, 1988.

D McCracken, Beyond the Glynns: The Phenomenon of the Giant's Causeway in Georgian Ireland,' *The Glynns,* Journal of the Glens of Antrim Historical Society, 13:21-25, 1985.

J H McGuigan, *The Giant's Causeway Tramway,* The Oakwood Press, 1964.

R Stenuit, *Treasures of the Armada,* David and Charles, 1972.

W M Thackeray, *The Irish Sketch Book of 1842,* Chapman Hall, London, 1843.

R M Young, 'Early Notices and Engraved Views of the Giant's Causeway', *Ulster Journal of Archaeology,* 3:40-49, 1897.

Chapter Seven:

R W G Carter and A J Parker (eds.) *Ireland: Contemporary perspectives on a land and its people*, Routledge, London and New York, 1989.

Department of Agriculture, Northern Ireland, *Countryside Management – the DANI Strategy*, 1990.

Department of the Environment, Northern Ireland, *Causeway Coast Area of Outstanding Natural Beauty, Guide to Designation*, 1989.

L Gallagher and D Rogers, *Castle, Coast and Cottage: The National Trust in Northern Ireland,* The Blackstaff Press, Belfast, 1986.

Northern Ireland Tourist Board, *Survey of Visitors to the Giant's Causeway*, 1980.

Causeway Coast Area of Outstanding Natural Beauty

The north coast of County Antrim, between Portrush and Ballycastle, including the Giant's Causeway, is one of the most spectacular coastlines in Europe. The Department of the Environment for Northern Ireland designated the Causeway Coast Area of Outstanding Natural Beauty in 1989. This designation formally recognises that the coast and adjacent farmland is a landscape of national importance. The purpose of designation is to help protect and where possible improve this landscape for the benefit of those living in the area and for the many visitors who come to see and enjoy its natural beauty.

Giant's Causeway – National Nature Reserve

The Giant's Causeway and 71 hectares of the adjacent coastline was designated as a National Nature Reserve in 1987 by the Department of the Environment for Northern Ireland. National Nature Reserves are managed specifically to conserve nature and to promote education and research. The Department works closely with the National Trust, who own and manage the reserve, to ensure that the site is protected and that visitors are given an opportunity to discover and enjoy the geological wonders and wildlife of the Causeway and surrounding cliffs.

Giant's Causeway – World Heritage Site

In 1986 the World Heritage Convention accepted the Giant's Causeway on to its list of sites and monuments. The Causeway meets two of the criteria for an outstanding natural property:

- It is a prime example of the earth's evolutionary history during the tertiary epoch.
- It contains rare and superlative natural phenomena.

The site also has outstanding cultural value in that it contains the wreck of the Girona, a nautical archaeological site associated with an event of international historical significance.

The World Heritage Convention seeks to promote international co-operation in the protection of sites which are of exceptional interest and of universal value.

Printed in the United Kingdom for HMSO
Dd 303880 C.60 7/92 55-9255 29254

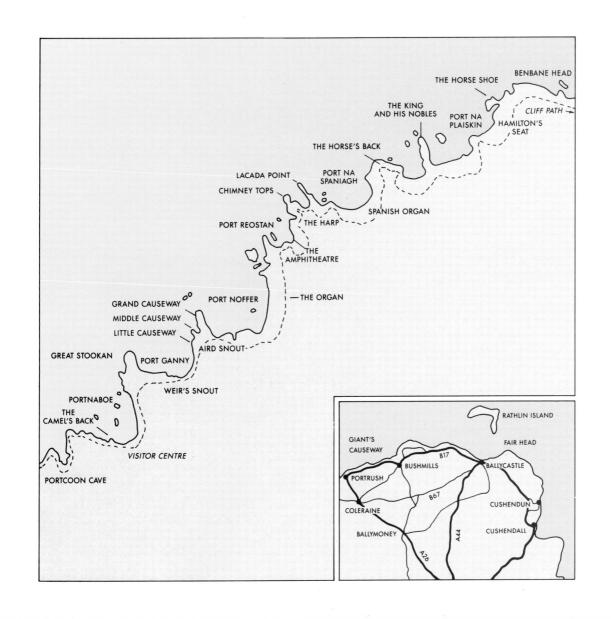

HMSO publications are available from:

HMSO Publications Centre
(Mail, fax and telephone orders only)
PO Box 276, London, SW8 5DT
Telephone orders 071-873 9090
General enquiries 071-873 0011
(queing system in operation for both numbers)
Fax orders 071-873 8200

HMSO Bookshops
16 Arthur Street, Belfast, BT1 4GD 0232 238451 Fax 0232 235401
49 High Holborn, London, WC1V 6HB (counter service only)
071-873 0011 Fax 071-873 8200
258 Broad Street, Birmingham, B1 2HE 021-643 3740 Fax 021-643 6510
Southey House, 33 Wine Street, Bristol, BS1 2BQ 0272 264306 Fax 0272 294515
9-21 Princess Street, Manchester, M60 8AS 061-834 7201 Fax 061-833 0634
71 Lothian Road, Edinburgh, EH3 9AZ 031-228 4181 Fax 031-229 2734

HMSO'S Accredited Agents
(see Yellow Pages)

and through good booksellers